Owls

Other titles in the Nature's Predators series include:

Owls

Karen D. Povey

KIDHAVEN PRESS

An imprint of Thomson Gale, a part of The Thomson Corporation

Detroit • New York • San Francisco • San Diego • New Haven, Conn.
Waterville, Maine • London • Munich

© 2005 Thomson Gale, a part of The Thomson Corporation.

Thomson and Star Logo are trademarks and Gale and KidHaven Press are registered
trademarks used herein under license.

For more information, contact
KidHaven Press
27500 Drake Rd.
Farmington Hills, MI 48331-3535
Or you can visit our Internet site at http://www.gale.com

LIBRARY OF CONGRESS CATALOGING-IN-PUBLICATION DATA

Povey, Karen D., 1962–
    Owls / by Karen Povey.
        p. cm. — (Nature's predators)
    Summary: Discusses the physical characteristics, behavior, and predators of
various owls.
    Includes bibliographical references and index.
    ISBN 0-7377-2349-1 (hardcover : alk. paper)
    1. Owls—Juvenile literature. I. Title. II. Series.
    QL696.S8P68 2005
    598.9'7—dc22
 	
                                                                2004016279

Printed in the United States of America

CONTENTS

CHAPTER ONE

Masters of the Night

When the sun goes down and darkness comes to the world's forests and fields, a fierce **predator** comes out of hiding to begin its hunt. Using its amazing senses and skills, the owl detects a meal and swoops down on its unsuspecting **prey**.

The owl is one of the most expert predators in the world, pursuing its prey under the cover of darkness. Nearly every feature of an owl's body and behavior equips it for its life as nighttime predator. The owl has extremely sharp vision and keen hearing to locate prey in near total darkness. Special feathers allow it to fly silently, taking prey by surprise. Large, powerful feet serve as the owl's highly efficient killing weapons.

The Raptors

Birds such as owls that catch and kill prey with their feet are called **raptors**. Like all raptors, owls have feet equipped with sharp claws, called **talons**, that help them grip and kill their prey. Raptors that hunt in the day, such as hawks, eagles, and falcons, also have powerful feet and talons. Although owls and daytime raptors look and behave similarly, they are not closely related to each other.

Owl Classification

To understand the relationships between different kinds of animals, scientists divide them into separate groups. Animals that share certain features are placed in the same groups and are considered to be close relatives. This system of grouping animals is called classification.

Because most owls are very similar, scientists classify them together in one large group, called an order. Owls are in the **Strigiformes** order. (Because they are not related to owls, the daytime raptors are classified in a different order.) Scientists believe there are over two hundred different kinds, or **species**, of owls. Because new species of owls continue to be discovered, this number may grow. The Strigiformes order is further divided into two smaller groups called families.

The family **Tytonidae** consists of the barn owls. Barn owls look slightly different from other owls. They are more slender and have heart-shaped faces. There are sixteen different species of barn owls. These are among the most common and widespread of the

There are more than two hundred owl species found throughout the world. Here, screech owlets cling to their perch.

world's owls. In fact, the common barn owl is found living in more places than any other bird in the world.

The remaining 189 owl species belong to the **Strigidae** family. Scientists refer to these as "typical" owls. This family includes owls ranging in size from the tiny elf owls of the southwestern United States to the huge eagle owls of Africa and Asia.

Owl Distribution

Owls live in nearly every corner of the world except for the Antarctic. Owls can be found in rain forests, grasslands, deserts, arctic tundra, remote ocean islands, and suburban backyards. The tropics of South

America, Asia, Africa, and Australia are home to the greatest numbers of different kinds of owls because of the large numbers of prey animals available there.

Owl Appearance

No matter where they live, all owls look very much alike and have a unique appearance easy to recognize. They have large, rounded heads, forward-facing eyes, and a short, curved beak. Some owls can appear quite

Owls, like this great horned owl, have lightweight bodies that are designed for flying.

large, but owls have surprisingly small bodies. A dense covering of soft, fluffy feathers makes them look much bigger than they really are. Even the largest owls, the eagle owls, weigh only about 6 pounds (2.7 kg). Most owls weigh much less, from 1 or 2 pounds (0.4 kg or 0.9 kg) down to just a few ounces.

Designed for Flight

Owls, like other flying birds, have special features that reduce their weight, making flight possible. Instead of having the dense, heavy bones that mammals do, an owl has mostly hollow and very lightweight bones. In fact, an owl's skeleton is so light that it actually weighs less than its feathers. In addition, owls have fewer bones than mammals. Many of the owl's bones are fused, or joined, and other bones are missing altogether, when compared to the similar bones in a mammal.

Although it is lightweight, an owl's skeleton is still extremely strong to withstand the forces of flying. The hollow bones have braces inside that function like the struts that strengthen the wing of an airplane. A large, sturdy breastbone serves as an anchor for the strong muscles that power the owl's wings.

The owl's skeleton also plays an important role in helping it breathe while flying. As in other flying birds, an owl's lungs are connected to the hollow air spaces in its bones as well as to other air sacs through-out its body. This system allows an owl to move large amounts of oxygen through its body while flying in pursuit of prey.

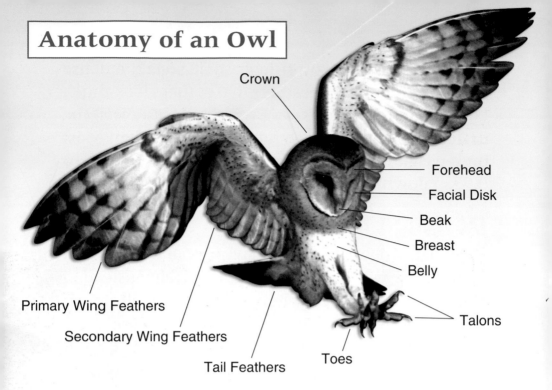

Crown

Forehead

Facial Disk

Beak

Breast

Belly

Primary Wing Feathers

Talons

Secondary Wing Feathers

Tail Feathers

Toes

Owl Feathers

Another important feature that helps owls fly are their feathers. Owls have two main types of feathers, each with a special purpose. The feathers that cover the outside of an owl's body, including the wing and tail feathers, are called contour feathers. These feathers are used in flight and also protect the owl from wind and rain. Buried underneath the contour feathers are the fluffy down feathers that trap air against the owl's body to keep it warm.

Owls spend a great deal of time grooming their feathers to keep them clean and properly arranged. This process is called **preening**. Owls have a special gland at the base of their tails that gives off an oily substance. When an owl preens its feathers, it uses its beak to spread this oil over its feathers to protect them and make them waterproof.

Compared to many other birds, owls have feathers that are fairly drab—usually brown, gray, or reddish-brown. These colors provide **camouflage** for owls,

A barn owl grooms, or preens, its feathers to keep them clean and neatly arranged.

helping them to stay hidden by allowing them to blend into their surroundings. For example, owls that live in forests often have mottled feathers that match the bark of the trees in which they perch. In contrast, the snowy owl is almost totally white. This allows the snowy owl to blend into its arctic environment.

Staying hidden is important because an owl's success as a predator depends on its ability to take prey by surprise. However, before it can catch a meal an owl must first find suitable prey to hunt.

CHAPTER TWO

Silent Hunters

Owls hunt and catch many different kinds of animals. In general, owls of similar size usually hunt similar types of prey. Small owls, such as pygmy owls and screech owls, mainly catch large insects such as grasshoppers and beetles. These owls may also hunt lizards, mice, and small birds.

Medium-sized owls, such as barn owls, the spotted owl, or Europe's tawny owl, hunt many different kinds of small animals. Rodents, such as rats, mice, and squirrels, are most frequently on their menu, but these owls may also hunt snakes, frogs, birds, rabbits, and bats.

The largest owls hunt the largest prey. The great horned owl and the eagle owls of Europe, Africa, and Asia are well known for being fierce predators. In addition to hunting rodents and other small animals, these birds also kill skunks, deer fawns, monkeys, other owls, and young eagles. While most large owls eat many different kinds of food, some hunt just a few types of prey. For example, there are six species of fish owls in Asia and Africa that eat little besides

Owls hunt many different kinds of prey. Here, a hungry screech owl devours a hornworm.

the fish, crabs, and crayfish they catch from rivers and lakes.

Super Sight

Nature has equipped owls with sharp senses for locating and catching their prey in the dark. Like most predators, owls have eyes located at the front of their heads. This allows the vision from each eye to overlap, providing the owl with what is called **binocular vision**. Binocular vision allows a predator to judge distances accurately when attacking prey. In contrast, prey animals usually have eyes on the sides of their heads. As a result, they lack binocular vision but have a wider field of view for spotting danger.

An owl's eyes are very sensitive and need only a small amount of light from the stars or moon to function. Owls can see from ten to one hundred times better than a person can at night. To gather as much light as possible, owl eyes are extremely large. In fact, some owls have eyes that are bigger than their brains!

Because an owl's eyes are so large, they are shaped differently from those of other animals to fit into the skull. Instead of being ball-shaped, they are shaped like long tubes. Because of this shape, they cannot move freely within the eye sockets like human eyes do. Therefore, an owl cannot see very much at the sides of its body. If an owl wants to look at something not directly to the front, it must turn its head to see.

To make up for this limited field of view, owls have extremely flexible necks. While humans have seven neck bones, owls have fourteen. Owl neck bones rotate much more freely than humans', allowing the bird to turn its head over three-quarters of the way around. With this ability, an owl can sit quietly on its perch, with very little movement that might reveal its presence, and look around for prey.

Day-Hunting Owls

Because owls see very well at night, people often assume that their vision is poor during the day. This is not true. During daylight, owls see as well as most other birds. Furthermore, not all owls hunt at night. Many are most active at dawn and dusk, while others, such as the snowy owl and burrowing owl, hunt mostly during the day.

Owl Hearing

Despite the owl's well-deserved reputation for having excellent eyesight, the main sense most owls use while hunting is actually their hearing. Most owls capture prey that is often hidden under grass, snow, or leaves. These animals, such as small rodents, would not usually be visible to an owl on the hunt. So instead of using its eyes, an owl uses its sensitive hearing to detect a target scurrying along undercover. Owls have several features that allow them to have such astonishing hearing ability.

The most visible feature of an owl's hearing system is the special arrangement of feathers around its face, called the facial disk. These feathers form a cup-shaped ruff that helps to catch sound and channel it to the owl's ears. This works in much the same way as a person cupping a hand over his or her ear to better hear a faint sound. An owl can change the shape of its facial disk to better trap the sound it hears.

A snowy owl sitting on a perch twists its head around in search of prey.

An owl's ears are not visible on the outside of its body. Some owls have feathers called ear tufts on the tops of their heads, but these tufts have no function in hearing. Instead, an owl's ears are large, open slits on the sides of its head. The shape and size of the ears vary depending on the species of owl. Owls such as barn owls that prey almost exclusively on hidden rodents have the largest ear openings.

The position of an owl's ears can also vary. Some owls have ears that are in different places on each side

The feathers on the owl's face are designed to channel sound to the ears on the sides of its head.

of their heads. That is, one ear is located higher than the other. With this difference, sound will arrive at one ear a split second earlier than at the other ear. This difference allows an owl to determine exactly where a sound originates and therefore where the prey is located.

Surprise Attack

Once an owl has located a potential target, it must be able to take that prey by surprise to make a successful kill. To do this, most owls have special feathers that allow them to fly silently. When other birds fly, their stiff feathers rub against each other, creating sound. The soft, fluffy feathers of an owl, however, make virtually no noise during flight.

In addition, the front edges of the flight feathers on an owl's wings have tiny fringes instead of being smooth. These fringes silence the flow of air over the wings during flight. As a result, an owl can swoop toward its prey with complete surprise. Owls that hunt fish do not have fringed flight feathers since fish are not able to hear the birds' approach.

On the Hunt

Most owls live and hunt within a certain area, called a territory. An owl will defend its territory by chasing away other owls of the same species that may pass through. By protecting its territory, an owl protects its food source. Within this territory, an owl will have certain places where it prefers to hunt.

An owl's special feathers are designed so the owl's prey cannot hear the swooping, surprise approach.

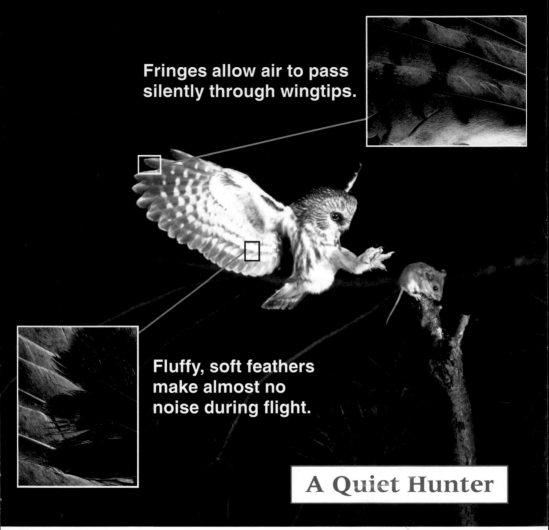

Fringes allow air to pass silently through wingtips.

Fluffy, soft feathers make almost no noise during flight.

A Quiet Hunter

Most owls do not spend much time flying while hunting. Instead, owls usually sit on a perch, looking and listening for prey. Owls usually have favorite perching spots from which they like to hunt. These perches may be low branches, tree stumps, or fence posts. Once on a perch, the owl will hold its body perfectly still, turning only its head to search for prey.

When an owl sees or hears a potential meal, it will quickly pounce down upon it.

A few species of owls will pursue their prey more actively instead of hunting with this "wait and pounce" approach. The long-eared owl uses slow, gliding flights to skim very low over the ground while searching for rodents. The great horned owl is known for diving at squirrel nests to flush the occupants into the open where it can grab them. Owls that eat insects often dive through the swarms of bugs attracted by streetlights.

No matter how it hunts, an owl is a serious threat for the prey animals in its territory. Once it identifies a target, the owl uses deadly accuracy to swoop down for the kill.

CHAPTER THREE

Owl Appetites

An owl on the attack flies toward its prey with its feet trailing behind to make a smooth approach. Just before impact, the owl swings it legs and feet forward in preparation for making the kill. At this time, it also closes its eyes to protect them from harm. The owl strikes with its powerful feet and sharp talons, grasping its prey tightly. The owls's grip is so strong that its long talons slice right through the prey animal's body. Usually the prey dies instantly as its internal organs are pierced. If the prey is still alive, the owl uses its sharp beak to bite through the neck of the animal and quickly finish it off.

Although all raptors use their feet as deadly weapons, only owls have a special feature that gives them an advantage when attacking prey. Instead of having three toes facing the front and one toe facing behind (like the other raptors), owls have flexible outer toes that can change position. As a result, an owl can strike its prey with two toes facing forward and two toes facing back. This arrangement results in a deadly trap of talons that is almost impossible to escape.

Fishing Owls

This special toe arrangement also helps fishing owls gain a secure hold on a wriggling fish. To provide an

A screech owl grips a frog in its talons, which are sharp enough to pierce through the frog's body.

even better grip, fishing owls have rough bumps, called **spicules**, on the bottom of their feet. These owls are among the few species that do not have feathers on their lower legs or feet. Some fishing owls hunt by pouncing from a perch near a river's edge. Others, however, will wade into the water and grab passing fish, frogs, or crabs with their feet.

Snow Hunters

Not even the cover of deep snow can protect animals from an owl's lethal talons. Owls that hunt in northern areas, such as the great gray owl or snowy owl, are able to find and catch rodents that live in burrows beneath the snow. Once they hear a target, these owls will plunge through the snow, feet first, to catch their prey. Owls that live in these cold climates have dense feathers protecting their feet and toes. Owls living in warmer regions have feet with much sparser feathers.

Mealtime

Once an owl makes a kill, it is very wary and constantly watches for other predators or animals that may try to steal its food. To reduce these threats, an owl usually eats its prey as quickly as possible. Smaller prey is eaten on the spot, gulped down whole. Larger prey is carried in the owl's feet or beak back to a **roost**, or resting site, and eaten in pieces. Owls often eat the heads of their prey first. Next, they usually remove the intestines and stomach before eating the rest of the animal in large chunks.

A great gray owl pounces on a rodent in a burrow beneath the snow.

Digesting Dinner

Because owls eat their prey whole or in very large pieces, their bodies have ways to cope with the indigestible parts such as fur, feathers, and bones that enter their digestive systems. When an owl eats, acid produced by its stomach dissolves the soft parts of the meal. These dissolved parts are passed through the digestive system and absorbed as nutrients by the intestines.

The indigestible parts of the meal remain trapped in a portion of the owl's stomach called the gizzard. In the gizzard, the fur and bones of the owl's meal are compressed to form a pellet. About ten hours after eating a meal, the owl regurgitates, or spits up, the pellet. The pellet is covered in a coating of mucous so it

A pygmy owl swallows a lizard whole. Later, the owl will spit up the indigestible parts of its prey.

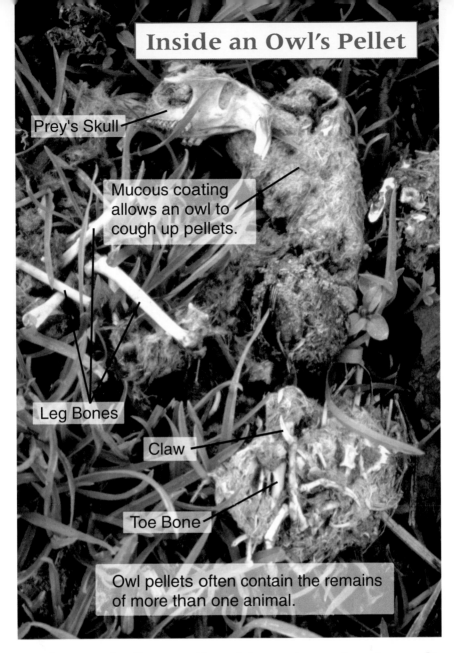

Inside an Owl's Pellet

Prey's Skull

Mucous coating allows an owl to cough up pellets.

Leg Bones

Claw

Toe Bone

Owl pellets often contain the remains of more than one animal.

can be coughed up easily without damaging the owl's throat. Most owls expel two pellets each day.

The pellet contains the indigestible contents from one meal, but that meal may have consisted of several different animals. Remains of animals that are eaten within a few hours of one another will be combined into one pellet. One researcher examining snowy owl pellets discovered the remains of twenty-seven meadow voles in a single pellet. Owls usually expel the pellets while they are perched at their favorite roost. As a result, the ground beneath the roost is often littered with the remains of hundreds of the owl's meals.

Feast or Famine

The amount of time an owl spends hunting and the number of meals it eats may vary considerably. Small owls, such as the insect-eating species, spend a great deal of time hunting because their prey is very small. They must eat frequent meals and hunt nearly all night long to find enough food.

Larger owls may spend less time hunting, but often follow a regular schedule. Barn owls, for example, may hunt two to three times each night. The first hunt takes place just after dark, the second near midnight, and the third just before dawn. Owls that hunt large prey, such as the eagle owls, need to hunt less frequently if they make a kill that provides all the food they need for the night.

Owls spend the most time hunting when they are raising young. Because young owls grow rapidly, their parents must hunt almost constantly. In just one breeding season, a pair of barn owls may kill fifteen hundred rodents to feed themselves and their young. Elf owls have been seen bringing food to the nest at the rate of one insect each minute during the peak of their chicks' growth.

Sometimes, however, food is not always plentiful for owls. Snowy owls in the Arctic, especially, face food shortages when rodent populations drop or the weather is especially severe. At these times, snowy owls will leave their territories and fly south in search of food.

Caching Food

Sometimes an owl will catch more food than it can eat in a single meal. This may happen if there is a large amount of prey easily available. For instance, owls have been observed hunting large numbers of animals

Barn owls hunt several times each night. Here, a barn owl flies with a rodent in its bill.

fleeing from wildfires or floods. When an owl has eaten its fill, it will store food for later use. This habit is called **caching** (CASH-ing). An owl may cache food in tree branches or under logs, leaves, or snow.

Owls will also cache food in the nest when they are feeding young. Storing extra food at the nest will help a pair of owls feed its chicks if they are unable to find food due to bad weather or an unsuccessful hunt. Even with this precaution, however, owls are not always successful in catching enough prey to keep themselves and their young alive.

CHAPTER FOUR

Owl Enemies

Although owls are superb predators, they may sometimes become prey themselves. Large owls are usually safe from other hunting animals, but on occasion may be killed by eagles or wild cats. Small owls have more predators, including hawks, falcons, larger owls, foxes, and snakes.

Staying Safe

An owl resting at its roost may find itself in danger if it is discovered by a predator. Although owls have some ways to defend themselves when attacked, their best defense is to avoid being noticed. Therefore, an owl will choose a roost where it can remain well hidden. Usually an owl will select a hiding spot in dense brush, a hollow tree, or in a nook on a canyon wall. Owls that live in areas without trees or cliffs, such as snowy owls or short-eared owls, will rest on the ground, hidden in clumps of grass.

Once at its roost, an owl will position itself to take best advantage of its camouflage. A screech owl, for example, may sit among a tangle of branches that

Mountain lions are one type of wildcat that preys on owls.

matches its feathers, making it almost impossible to detect. While roosting, an owl will often raise its ear tufts. These feathers will break up the shape of the owl's round body, helping it to better blend with the surrounding branches or look like a broken-off tree limb.

Away from the Mob

Despite an owl's excellent camouflage, sometimes other animals will find it. Often, owls are discovered by songbirds or crows that live in the same area. When that happens, large groups of these birds will gather near the owl's roost in a behavior called mobbing. Mobbing birds will torment the owl by swooping around it in wave after wave of attackers. These birds will sometimes even strike the owl on its head or back with their claws. During this attack, the birds will also sound their loud alarm calls.

These mobbing attacks do not harm the owl. Instead, they serve mostly to alert other birds in the area that the owl is there. In some cases, the owl remains at its roost while it is being mobbed. Other times, the owl escapes the mob by flying a short distance to another roost. Owls usually do not attack birds that are mobbing them.

Fight or Flight

Besides being discovered by mobbing birds, sometimes an owl is found by a predator. When that happens, the owl usually remains still or slowly stretches its body into a tall, thin position in a last-ditch attempt to hide.

Threatened by an attacker, an owl spreads its wings to appear large and frightening.

At the same time, it keeps its large eyes hidden by peeking at its enemy through barely open lids.

If the enemy approaches too closely, the owl will give up trying to hide and use a different tactic. Sometimes an owl attempts to dash quickly into flight and escape. Most owls, however, stay in place and threaten their attackers. Owls use what is called a threat display to make themselves appear large and frightening to predators. During this display, an owl will puff out all its feathers, lift and open its wings, and spread its tail feathers. The owl will also sway its head while hissing and clacking its beak. By helping the owl look fierce, this threat display works well to scare off a possible attacker.

Vulnerable Young

Even very young owls still in the nest use this threat display. Adult owls defend their young fiercely, but if a nestling owl's parents are away, it is in danger of attack by almost any predator that can reach the nest. Baby owls will clack their beaks furiously at intruders. The loud sound that results will often alert their parents to the danger, bringing them back to the nest to protect the chicks.

Young owls may be harmed by predators, but they also face other serious threats as they grow up. Once they leave the nest, young owls must learn to hunt and set up their own territories. Because they are inexperienced at flying and hunting and are not familiar with their new homes, these owls stand a much

A female grey owl feeds her babies in the nest while the male watches for danger.

greater chance of dying than adult owls do. Scientists estimate that 50 percent to 70 percent of owls die before they reach their first birthday. These deaths are due to starvation, predators, or accidents while hunting or flying.

Human Threats to Owls

Accidents are also a serious threat to adult owls. Many of the most common accidents that injure or kill owls are a result of the changes that people make to the owl's environment. Owls have been found entangled in barbed-wire fences, electrocuted by power lines, or killed after crashing into windows.

Many owls are also killed in auto collisions. Open spaces around roads and highways create good hunting **habitat** for owls. Low-flying owls in these areas, however, are at extreme risk of being struck by cars. Scientists studying this problem have seen stretches of road where as many as thirteen owls were killed by cars in a single night.

Another serious threat to owls is the common practice of controlling mice and rats through the use of pesticides. Owls may eat rodents that have consumed pesticides and become poisoned themselves. In some areas, the use of these pesticides has caused the numbers of some owls, such as barn owls, to drop dramatically.

Today, most poisoning of owls is accidental, but owls were once considered pest animals and were often killed on purpose. In the past, farmers viewed owls as

This barn owl died after being caught in a trap. Farmers used to trap owls to stop them from preying on livestock.

livestock predators and routinely trapped and shot them. This view of owls as pests has changed dramatically in recent times. Most farmers now have a better understanding and appreciation for the important role owls play in controlling wild rodent populations that can damage crops. Some farmers now even try to attract owls by setting up nest boxes on their land.

Losing Ground

Today, most people admire owls and would never harm them on purpose. However, many species of owls have suffered large drops in numbers because of human activity. As human populations grow, the wild habitat that owls need to survive continues to shrink. Every year all over the world more homes are built, more forests are cleared, and more grasslands

A scientist handles an eagle owl to learn how best to protect the animal.

are converted to farmland. These changes mean that owls have fewer hunting grounds, fewer roost sites, and fewer places safe for nesting.

One owl especially threatened by loss of habitat is the endangered northern spotted owl, found in the Pacific Northwest of the United States. The northern spotted owl lives only in the ancient fir and cedar forests along the region's coast. Logging of these valuable trees has greatly reduced the size of the forest areas that can provide homes to these owls.

The Future of Owls

The plight of the northern spotted owl is well known because it has been the subject of much scientific study. However, almost nothing is known about many of the other species of owls around the world. Most owls living in the tropical forests of Asia or South America, for example, have never been studied at all. As a result, scientists are unsure if their populations are safe or declining.

With continued research, scientists hope to gain a greater understanding of how to protect owls. With this understanding, plans can be developed to make sure that owls will always be free to swoop silently over the world's forests and fields in search of their prey.

GLOSSARY

binocular vision: The ability to see through both eyes at once in order to accurately judge distances.

caching: Storing food for later use.

camouflage: The ability to blend into the surrounding environment to hide from predators or prey.

habitat: The environment in which an animal lives.

predator: An animal that hunts and kills other animals.

preening: The process of grooming feathers.

prey: An animal hunted and eaten by another animal.

raptors: Birds that hunt using powerful feet and sharp claws known as talons. Raptors include owls, hawks, falcons, and eagles.

roost: A place where a bird perches to rest.

species: A category of scientific classification used to label and identify groups of related plants or animals.

spicules: The bumps on the bottom of a fishing owl's feet that help it to grip prey.

Strigidae: The scientific name for the family of owls consisting of the "typical owls."

Strigiformes: The scientific name for the animal group, or order, made up of all of the owl species.

talons: The sharp claws a raptor uses to catch and hold prey.

Tytonidae: The scientific name for the family of owls consisting of the barn owls.

FOR FURTHER EXPLORATION

Books

Virginia Alvin and Robert Silverstein, *The Spotted Owl.* Brookfield, CT: Millbrook, 1994. This book discusses the threats to the spotted owl, the reasons for its decline, and the methods used for studying the species.

Kim Long, *Owls: A Wildlife Handbook.* Boulder, CO: Johnson, 1998. This book, including owl senses, hunting behavior, and owl folklore, serves as an excellent overview of the natural history of owls.

Helen Roney Sattler, *The Book of North American Owls.* New York: Clarion, 1995. This book provides an overview of the twenty-two species of North American owls. Scientifically accurate watercolor illustrations depict the lives and behavior of these owls.

Web Sites

The Hungry Owl Project (www.hungryowl.org). This organization promotes the use of barn owls as natural pest control to reduce the use of pesticides. Visit the site for information on building or buying owl nest boxes.

Owling.com (www.owling.com.) This Web site focuses on watching the wild owls of North and Central America. The site also includes photos, video, and audio tracks of owl calls.

The Owl Pages (www.owlpages.com). This Web site is full of information on owl behavior, biology, and owl conservation. Visit the site for a complete listing of the world's owl species and links for learning more.

INDEX

ABOUT THE AUTHOR

Karen D. Povey has spent her career as a conservation educator, working to instill an appreciation for wildlife in people of all ages. Karen makes her home in Tacoma, Washington, where she manages and presents live animal education programs at Point Defiance Zoo & Aquarium. Her work at the zoo involves caring for a variety of owl species, from a tiny screech owl to an enormous eagle owl, and sharing these popular birds with zoo visitors.